CLOSING

——THE——

GAP

A SIMPLE BLUEPRINT FOR TRANSFORMING YOUR LIFE

SEAN O'SHEA

ISBN: 978-0-692-98728-5

Cover by Mitransh Singh Parihar
mitransh_parihar@yahoo.com

Front cover photograph by Alison Turner
Back cover photograph by Laura Morgan

Edited by Gidget Hall / Waypoint Copywriting
https://waypointcopywriting.com

Designed by Mike Eiman
contact@mikeeiman.com

Audiobook production by Micheal Ziants / Airlift Productions
mike@airliftproductions.com

Contents

{ Introduction:
The Gap

Why do so many of us struggle? Why do so many of us live a life far below our potential?

Is it that we don't care enough or are too lazy? Are we not bright enough or talented enough?

I don't think so.

I think we all want more from life and from ourselves. I also think we're all capable of creating a far greater life than what we're currently living.

So if we want more, and we're capable of more, what's the problem? Why are so many of us still stuck?

Missing information.

When it comes to the skills, tools, and insights needed to lead an exceptional life, most of us are terribly under-informed.

If we're lucky, we might get the basics. Work hard, save money, be a nice person.

Unfortunately, some don't even get that. But the truth is, these basics, while super important, aren't nearly enough to create a great life.

To create a truly inspiring, powerful, enjoyable, and impactful life, we need more than just the basics.

We need a much deeper understanding of the human mind, how it works, and how it processes. We need to know how it can help or harm us, and how we can harness its power to create the reality we want.

Could the gap between your current reality and the life you want to live be totally dependent on what you feed your mind, what you believe, and the actions you take?

You betcha.

Could misconnecting one wire on a Ferrari cause it to go from an amazing machine of speed and jaw-dropping performance to an immobile, largely useless hunk of metal?

You betcha.

Here's the thing: you and that Ferrari aren't all that different. You both can do amazing things. But you both must be wired right to do them.

My Story

I come from a background of childhood divorce, alcoholism, and emotional, physical, and sexual trauma.

From an early age, I struggled with a host of learning disabilities, as well as mental hurdles such as OCD, social anxiety, and depression.

My life experiences included family violence, police visits, eviction notices, and food stamps. One unforgettable memory includes trips to the local mental institution to visit a step-parent receiving complimentary care for alcohol abuse.

That sounds rough, but life wasn't all bad. There were plenty of beautiful, wonderful, amazing times to remember as well. But I share this "hit list" of the ugly so you can know where I've come from—so you can know I've come by the breakthroughs and insights I'm sharing in this book honestly.

What followed my early life were years of struggle. I barely made it out of high school. From there I bounced from place to place, largely dependent on others to keep a roof over my head and food on the table.

I worked several "high profile" jobs during those years. I was a "fish boy" at the market. I was an overnight floor cleaner and a retail clothing clerk. I worked as a record store employee for ten years, and as a valet, parking cars for another ten.

None of these gigs were necessarily bad, but the older I got, the less "good" they became. When you're a record store clerk in your 30s, or parking cars five days a week when you're 40, for $10 an hour, that's pretty telling that things aren't going so well.

So there I was, forty years old. I lived in a tiny, 500-square-foot apartment. I drove a hand-me-down truck with no insurance. My relationships were a toxic disaster. My credit was toast.

I was broke, in debt, and borrowing money to get by. I was spiritually and emotionally at my lowest. My character and integrity were non-existent. Cheating, lying, and stealing? They all barely registered in my mind as flaws.

So what happened? How did I get here? I'd always believed I was meant for something special. Don't many of us? Don't we all?

How did someone with so much promise and potential get so far behind and become such a mess?

Remember that whole Ferrari metaphor earlier? Yeah, that was me—totally miswired. Miswired by my early experiences, by everything else I'd taken in over the course of my life, and by everything I'd missed.

Like so many who are struggling, I was missing critical pieces of information. Information that, if understood and applied, could have changed the entire landscape and trajectory of my life.

Because the truth is, even with all the challenges I started out with, there was plenty I could have done differently. And I knew it.

About this time in my life, a friend's experience helped me begin to learn how.

My friend was also a fellow searcher and struggler. I'd seen her making new choices and taking back control of her life. I trusted her, and I saw things were changing for her—for the better.

I dove into the authors and speakers she recommended. Names like Jim Rohn, Jack Canfield, Tony Robbins, Zig Ziglar, and more.

Unlike many of the other books and people I'd looked into before, there was something else here—something that rang of truth. There was a certain continuity in the messages.

I began to work my butt off to study and pull as much as I could from this handful of mentors. It wasn't easy for me at first. With my learning disabilities, every book (heck, every paragraph!) seemed to take forever for me to get through.

But I pushed on. I was learning so much. The ideas and concepts being thrown around made so much sense that I became obsessed.

It took time, but even the little shifts I began to achieve felt amazing. I was starting to see everything differently. I was seeing possibilities instead of limitations. I was seeing my power rather than just my blocks.

But mostly, I was seeing a world I'd completely missed.

And what was it that I'd missed? What was it that had kept me blocked and locked and struggling? Yep, information. Something as simple as that had derailed me for most of my life.

Flash forward just about ten years from that time, and boy, how things have changed.

I started a business. Then I started another, and then another.

I started writing and sharing my thoughts and finding they were connecting with others. I started teaching and mentoring.

Through consistent work, I completely overhauled my mindset. And, strangely enough, I overhauled my entire life in the process.

Jim Rohn once famously said, "If you will change, everything will change for you." And let me tell you, Jim was right.

Your Story

This book isn't intended to be a comprehensive, end-all, be-all. I have intentionally left it very sparse and open.

The goal is for this to be a framework and launching pad for you—the spark that sets you on a path of personal discovery and growth.

This book is meant to plant the seeds and get you thinking. But the hard work of digging in and finding your own answers will be up to you.

What you hold is the information I wished I'd had so many years ago.

This book covers the essential building blocks, the themes of success, that I found over and over again as I studied hundreds of books, videos, and mentors.

My goal for this book is that it (and the resources listed later) will help you discover your own answers, wherever you find yourself on this journey. I want it to help you avoid the pitfalls that trap so many good people, and keeps them stuck—living small, safe, unrealized lives.

My wish is that through these simple concepts, you will find your way to your own new story. A story of beauty, empowerment, wisdom, self-love, prosperity, generosity, happiness, and impact.

I promise, even if any of this feels impossible, crazy, or out of reach—it's not. It once felt the same way for me.

Trust me, if I can do it, anyone can.

These are the principles and concepts I found most helpful in transforming my own disabling story. I happily pass them on now to you.

P.S. The ten principles covered in this book are those I found most helpful. But there are many more principles, and many other ways to view this process. I encourage you to start here, get your foundation, and then dive into the resources listed in the back of the book. This is where you will find your deepest development.

I also recommend you return to these ten principles to help you remain grounded if you ever feel overwhelmed. You can't go wrong with these; they're the Big Kahunas.

1 Influence: Where It All Starts

> *"You are the average of the five people you spend the most time with."* — **Jim Rohn**

Most personal development starts with your thought process.

Your thoughts create your beliefs, which then determine your actions. So that seems to make sense. But, there's another step before all that. One that's often missed.

What goes into creating those thoughts, that then create your beliefs and actions?

Your influences.

What you feed your mind—through family, friends, school, church, co-workers, TV, radio, movies, books, and the Internet—determines your thoughts.

If we want to control our thoughts and beliefs and ensure we take the right actions based on them, we first have to control our influences. We have to go back one step further.

Most of us just allow what comes our way to come our way. We get caught up in group-think, herd mentality, fear-mongering, and gossip.

We wallow in toxic thoughts about the government, the economy, crime, possibility, wealth, health, human nature, and our own power—or lack of it.

We hear and see and read story after story of what's wrong, what's missing, why we can't, why we're better off staying safe instead of reaching for more.

These stories permeate our thoughts and eventually become beliefs.

And whatever we believe, we act on.

Understanding this, it's easy to see why it's imperative that we become acutely aware of our influences—in all their forms—and how they're affecting us.

Are they lifting us up or tearing us down? Helping us to see the upside, or reminding us of the downside? Are they bringing out our best or encouraging our worst?

We like to think we're less susceptible and less vulnerable to our surroundings, but we're intensely social creatures, and we are all too easily influenced by those around us.

Once you truly get this, everything else gets a whole lot easier. Everything starts to make a lot more sense. Your choices, your mistakes, your struggles, your tendencies, your strengths, your weaknesses.

Yep, they all started with your influences—from your earliest messages to the people you hang out with currently, to the stuff your brain has consumed and continues to consume.

The great news is, if you're ready to turn things around, there's no shortage of helpful, inspiring, and wise influences for you to pull from.

These influences can be real or virtual, alive or dead. Your closest group of advisors and influences could all live in books or videos (mine did!), so you are not at all limited by your current surroundings or environment.

With the Internet, we all have endless access to free (or nearly free) resources that can dramatically impact and change the course of our lives for the better.

But it's up to you to take ownership of this opportunity. You have to be prepared to do the hard work of monitoring, evaluating, and then vetting your influences—all of them, even those closest to you.

It won't be easy, but it'll likely be the most important work you'll ever do.

Action Step

Take a comprehensive inventory of all your influences and the way they make you think and feel about life, possibilities, and yourself. Do you feel encouraged, empowered, and proud, or discouraged, insecure, and ashamed?

Take responsibility for who and what you allow into your world. Only you have the power to control this. If there's negative stuff in your life, you've allowed it—and you can change it.

Systematically remove (or greatly reduce) your exposure to any negative or toxic influences and replace them with healthy, positive, empowering ones.

Don't be afraid to do a complete overhaul. And don't allow anyone to guilt or manipulate you for prioritizing your life, your growth, your future.

My Experience

I didn't understand any of this. I blindly took on whatever messages and stories and programming that were passed onto me and that surrounded me.

I bought into all the stories of limitation (lack of opportunity, happiness, wealth, etc.), personal value (what I was worth, what I deserved, what I was capable of), and what was and wasn't possible (think smaller, safer, more practical).

I took on the negative messages about people, society, money, and success. Meaning, I learned to view them all suspiciously through a toxic lens.

Because I had nothing positive to share, I, like many others, learned to connect through toxicity. Negative talk and gossip about other people and life became my primary connection tool.

My overall attitude and outlook on life (and myself) was horribly broken and unhealthy. It crippled my thoughts and beliefs, and of course, my actions.

That's how you end up a broken-down valet at age 40.

When I finally woke up (thanks to new influences!) and discovered who was at the center of this toxic universe (me), I went to work, and I went all in! I became deadly serious about ALL of my influences.

I began a determined and thorough removal of all negative or toxic people and things from my life. I removed friends, family, acquaintances, social media "friends," TV, books, movies ... anything that wasn't moving my mind in the right direction.

It was incredibly difficult at first, but then, I started to gain some momentum. I slowly felt my mind start to shift. I noticed I was becoming happier, lighter, more optimistic, more caring, more supportive, more creative.

I also noticed I was becoming less "edgy," less judgmental, less angry, less blaming, less toxic. I started seeing possibilities—and hope—everywhere.

This new view of the world and of myself inspired me.

For the first time, I saw a glimpse of a brighter, more fulfilling path. A new way to view life.

It caused me to work harder and dig deeper. I was determined to build a new and better me. A more valuable me. Someone I could actually be proud of.

I discovered an unexpected benefit of these new influences, too. Without my consciously realizing it, they had set a new bar for my behavior and beliefs. Things I would have been okay with before, I couldn't fathom now.

Dishonesty, gaming the system, gaining at the expense of another, or being self-consumed—these behaviors were no longer acceptable to me. This new virtual peer group was actually changing my character and personal values.

Amazing.

Changing my influences changed everything, and I do mean everything. This single step of becoming hyper-aware of who had access to my world, and controlling that access, started the life-changing process that led to everything else.

And I've never looked back!

2 100% Responsibility: Reclaiming Your Power

"Don't wish it was easier, wish that you were better. Don't wish for less problems, wish for more skills. Don't wish for less challenges, wish for more wisdom." —Jim Rohn

Okay, so what if after reading the first chapter you say something like, "But I can't help who my family is, what the government does, how the economy goes, what they teach in school, or that there's so much negativity on the news, the Internet, and in life."

You'd be right, and you'd be wrong.

Did you create all of your circumstances? No. Can you control all of your circumstances? No.

But you **CAN** decide how you react and respond to them. We can't always control our world, but we **CAN** control what we do about it.

This is where 100% responsibility comes in. It's a decision you make about the power you wish to have and the power you wish to give away. And it's one of the most important decisions you'll ever make.

Unfortunately, every day, people make the decision to be victims. They complain, blame, and give power to the circumstances of their lives.

Their job doesn't pay enough, their boss has it out for them, the economy stinks, and there are no opportunities. Their family is a disaster, the government is a mess, people always do them wrong, and all the good ones are taken. They're mentally or physically challenged in some fashion, and on and on.

And?

It's decision time.

Do you choose to allow these circumstances and beliefs to be your reality, or do you choose to create a reality that serves you?

Do you choose to be a victim or do you choose to be a victor?

It doesn't matter if these circumstances and beliefs are true or not, all that matters is the question of whether you want to be in control of your reality or whether you want your reality dictated to you.

As long as you believe things are beyond your control, being done to you, are unfair ... you and your life are stuck. You're powerless. You've become the victim.

Or you can make another choice.

The person who decides to take 100% responsibility makes a deal with themselves and the world. That deal is: It's all on them. The good, the bad, the ugly. And in exchange for that responsibility, that owning, they receive freedom, power, and control over their lives and state of mind.

Think about it. Once it's on you, you can change it. Once you own it, you're in control.

This is the magic pivot point that so many miss. They miss it because responsibility is hard. It means when things don't work, it's your fault. When you don't get that job, it's your fault. When you have relationship issues, it's your fault. When life is a mess, it's your fault.

No longer are things simply being done to you, things are being allowed by you. No longer are you being victimized by your circumstances, you're allowing your circumstances.

And that's where everything shifts!

By taking responsibility, fair or unfair, true or not, you take back control of your life. You hold yourself accountable to learn the skills, gain the tools, and develop yourself to make the changes necessary to succeed and thrive.

If you want the power to create what you want, the power to become who you want to be, the power to achieve what you want to achieve—regardless of where you've come from or what you've been through—then the trade-off and price of that empowerment is that you take 100% responsibility.

Trust me; it's the deal of a lifetime.

Action Step

Become hyper-aware of any moments where you slip into victim mode and start blaming or making excuses. As soon as you notice, shift your thinking, and find a way to take responsibility. (Also, start to recognize when others are playing the victim.)

Become a responsibility addict. Look for all the ways you could have affected a different outcome through different choices or actions. This can become a fun and challenging game. A game where no matter what occurs (or why) you work to find a creative way to take responsibility. Challenge yourself.

Turn the victim mindset upside down by owning everything, and watch how fast you shift from disempowered to empowered, from stuck to endless possibilities.

A special note: In situations truly beyond your control—childhood trauma, random violence, accidents, etc.—just know that while you were not responsible for what happened to you, you are responsible for how you respond and process these situations.

My Experience

Full disclosure, I was the "blame king!" I blamed everything and everyone around me. My family, my friends, my school, my learning and emotional issues, my early experiences, my bosses, my jobs, my pay, my city, the government, and on and on.

I was about as toxic and victim-y as you can get. I had a great story I could rattle off to anyone about all the injustices and sufferings of my life.

Everyone was to blame, except me. Everyone was at fault, except me. Everyone was responsible, except me.

And guess where that left me? Stuck, powerless and broken.

Had some tough stuff happened? Sure. Had it not been always easy? Of course. And???

And, as long as I bought and believed that victim story, I was guaranteed to remain exactly where I was.

It wasn't until I heard about this concept of 100% responsibility that I even knew there was a choice. I just assumed things were the way they were.

Of course, I resisted it at first—I was heavily invested in my story and victim identity—but over time I started to explore it a little. And then a little more.

Once I got the first taste of power and control over my life, I was intoxicated. I dove deeper and deeper.

Instead of feeling bad, like I thought it would, taking responsibility was completely liberating and empowering ... and exhilarating. I knew I was onto something special.

That's not to say it was easy. Old, deep habits and beliefs die hard, so I had to watch myself like a hawk. But I was encouraged by my new influences to keep pushing and striving.

And so I did. And little by little I started to turn my victim mindset around. I worked hard to catch it every time it would start to creep out.

Pretty soon, I was in a new mode: the responsibility mode. I was actively looking for my part in whatever wasn't working. What could I have done differently? What could I have done better? What could I have changed to change the outcome?

These shifts in mindset and beliefs unlocked a new world for me. By looking for and owning everything I could, I found my power and I found my way out.

No longer would my circumstances or my story define me, or what I could or couldn't do. I would define them.

3 Goal Setting:
Setting & Getting Your Dreams

"You can't hit a target you cannot see,
and you cannot see a target you do not have." — **Zig Ziglar**

Another tried and true pillar in the world of personal development, and the world of the successful in general is goal setting.

And while you'd think this simple, life-changing concept would be understood and used by all of us, it's unfortunately not the case.

Of course, we use goal setting in its smaller forms all the time without thinking about it. We decide we want to go to dinner, we pick out the place, the time, how we'll get there, and voila, done. Goal achieved.

Or maybe we need a weekend getaway. We decide where we want to visit, what hotel we'll stay at, what sights we want to see, and we take the steps to organize it and make it happen. Once again, goal set, goal achieved.

Reading the above, it makes the whole goal setting thing seem pretty straight-forward—we know it works! So then how come so few of us actually use this same simple process for the big picture?

How come only a tiny percentage of us have actually sat down and written out, in detail, who we want to be, where we want to go, and what we want to achieve with our lives?

For most of us, we've never been clearly taught the value of goal setting. It's likely that our parents, family, and friends weren't taught, and never learned to use this practice either, so it's no surprise that it's foreign.

If we have heard about it, we've likely thought it was too difficult, or overwhelming, or uncomfortable to undertake.

We ask, "What will people think or say about my goals? What if I try and fail? What if I have no idea who or what I want to be and how to get there? What if it all just seems too complicated?"

Now we're getting to the root of why most people don't set goals.

It's uncomfortable, and it's work.

But the truth is, without harnessing the power of goal setting, people will bounce around aimlessly. Instead of being focused, on-task, and taking the steps needed to reach their goals and dreams, they'll just wander through life.

They'll achieve far less. They'll become far less. And they'll have far less.

All because they let this simple practice slip by them.

Sure it's going to take some work, and maybe even some mild discomfort. But compared to the work and discomfort of living a small, mediocre, directionless life, it's a breeze.

Let's start by breaking goal setting into three easy steps:

1. **Decide what you want.**
2. **Write it down.**
3. **Create small, daily steps toward achieving your goals.**

That's not so crazy or overwhelming, right?

To help you get a better handle on goal setting, and to show you how uncomplicated it really is, I'm going to share with you my own goal setting process. There are many approaches, but this works extremely well for me.

First, set aside a few hours of quiet time with a notebook or pad. Then, just let it all pour out. Don't hold anything back.

Nothing is too big, too small, too bold, too silly, or too crazy. Just unload. Don't worry about perfect—this list can always change. You're not married to any of these goals. (I do this master list once a year.)

Make sure you cover relationships, career, health, financial, fun, big projects, contribution, etc.

Now you've got your master list. From here I want you to narrow your goals down to just six. Pick a variety of super important goals that will enrich the entire scope of your life. Once the six are chosen, put the master list away.

On a new pad, which will become your daily companion, write your Big Six goals across the very top of the page with their corresponding numbers. (The brain tends to see whatever is listed first as being most important, so be conscious of your numbering.)

Then make two lists below.

The first is your "To-Do" list, which is filled with all the regular life stuff that needs to get done that day (laundry, post office, etc.). But, what makes **THIS** "To-Do" list special is that you also include among all the daily tasks at least **ONE** thing that advances each of your Big Six goals. Even if the **ONE** thing is just a super small step (which it usually is), there **HAS** to be something on the list, every day, that moves each of your big goals forward. (Double check before you start your day that each of the 6 has an action step written down.)

Next, under the "To-Do" list, on the same page, map out a "Soon" list. This list is just what it sounds like—it contains everything you need to get done soon. "Soon" could mean within a few days or a month or two.

This list contains various "life" stuff as well as future action plans for your Big Six goals. These are important things that you want written down and "captured" (so they're off your brain) but which you won't be able to get to immediately.

As items get crossed off the "To-Do" list, you'll replace them with something from the "Soon" list. And on and on.

What's great about this approach is that it keeps you on track with regular life responsibilities as well as consistently moving you forward, towards the bigger stuff in your life. All in one spot, and in a super simple, easy-to-maintain fashion.

The entire process takes about 10-15 minutes to do. You can do it before you go to bed or first thing in the morning.

Now, you can follow my approach, or you can develop your own. That's the cool thing about creating goals and action plans—there's really no wrong way—as long as you follow the basic rules: 1.) Decide what you want, 2.) Write it down, and 3.) Create small, daily steps towards achieving your goals.

As you work on this process, you'll start to see some fascinating things happen. You'll find unexpected people and opportunities popping up all over. Things you need to help you on your journey will "magically" appear. You'll swear something weird and cosmic is going on. But it's actually entirely practical and explainable.

Your brain has a filtering system. This system helps prevent your brain from being overloaded from the millions of stimuli in your environment. It can only process so much, so it has to create priorities. The brain filters out that which it deems unnecessary or unhelpful, and it filters in that which it deems beneficial and valuable.

And here's the thing, **YOU** set the filters! What you focus on and what you tell your mind is important and valuable is what it filters in. What you ignore or actively decide against, it filters out.

This, my friends, is the component of goal setting that most are unaware of. And it's actually the most powerful piece of the puzzle.

Once you realize you can control your brain's filters—to allow you to see possibilities and options and opportunities you otherwise wouldn't—you've bumped into the closest thing to magic there is.

This is why goal setting is something every successful person uses. It keeps you consciously focused on creating what you want, and it keeps you subconsciously focused as well.

Meaning, it gives you practical daily direction (make this call, take this action), while also tuning the deeper parts of your mind into being on the lookout for any helpful bits of information that can further your success and goal achievement.

Action Step

Take some time to really think about what you want to be, have, and contribute. What do you want your days to look like? Your career? Your family? Your finances? Your legacy?

This is your life, design it as you'd like it to be. If you don't, someone else will.

Keep the process and the concept simple. Don't let it become something more complicated than it is. We're simply making decisions about what we want, and figuring out how to get there. Keep it simple and have fun!

Also, don't be surprised if you feel a little silly or embarrassed writing big goals down. If dreaming big and aiming high is new to you (and your influences), be prepared to feel some resistance and anxiety about starting this process.

Regardless of the discomfort, be bold. You only get one life. Don't design a safe, small one that you'll regret later.

My Experience

To be perfectly honest, I'm not sure I'd ever truly heard about goal setting in any real sense. Of course, I'd heard about having a goal. But the idea of having a strategic plan of multiple life goals—consciously considered and written down—was completely foreign.

I had no idea that by using this simple process, I could stay on track and work on the small, but essential steps to create progress. So I just stumbled around. I didn't know small, consistent actions added up to big changes over time. Duh.

I also had zero awareness of any filtering system in my brain. I didn't know that I could control what my brain looked for and what it found. So of course, I missed seeing and finding people and opportunities that were right under my nose.

Once I learned about how goal setting worked, boy did things change.

I became meticulous about working towards the small and the large stuff on my list. I wrote it all out; I had fun dreaming of all the things I wanted to create and achieve.

But I also felt silly dreaming about a life that seemed so far from my current reality.

When you're parking cars for a living and barely getting by every month—or in really tough months, borrowing money to get by—dreaming of building a successful business, becoming someone who has a positive impact on others, and having all sorts of good stuff in my life seemed, well, kind of crazy.

Writing those first goals down seemed so ridiculous. But, because I was surrounding myself with influences who were all cheering me on, and who had all accomplished similar, and even greater feats, I gave it a shot.

What transpired shortly thereafter was mind blowing: Multiple businesses, homes in different cities, amazing new relationships, and connections with family and friends at much deeper levels. I'd built a positive reputation that was spreading, had money in the bank, enjoyed a totally different lifestyle, and discovered the ability to mentor and share my resources with others. Possibilities were everywhere, and I had a new-found sense of personal power.

Reviewing my old goals, it's almost freaky to see how many of them have come to pass, and in almost the exact fashion I envisioned them. Even things that seemed absolutely beyond possibility—crazy stuff I was sure was only meant for others—have somehow found their way to me.

Amazing.

That said, I've also adapted—and even let go of—many goals that, at the time, seemed incredibly important and right on the money, but later I realized weren't a good fit.

Be prepared to allow your goals to change and morph. I've outgrown certain goals and tweaked others as I've learned more about them (and me).

Life is always going to throw some major curveballs at us, so don't think of letting a goal go as some kind of failure. It might be the best thing you could do.

It's a balancing act of staying focused and on-course, while simultaneously being open to things shifting, becoming less important, or just in need of adjustment. I check in with myself often to make sure the goals I'm working on are still what the current version of me truly wants.

In short, goal setting—and a daily goal routine—has completely changed my life. It changed who I've been able to become, and it changed what I've been able to accomplish.

4 Habits: The Glue

"We are what we repeatedly do.
Excellence, then, is not an act, but a habit." — **Aristotle**

What makes up a life? A collection of moments. That's it really. It's a big collection, but it's still just a bunch of moments all strung together.

It's easy to get fooled into thinking something as amazing and grand as life would be governed by some far more profound structure. But as grand as it all might seem, and as profound as it all might feel, your life is still just a bunch of moments, a bunch of decisions, and a bunch of actions, all piled up.

Your direction, growth, and accomplishments will all be dictated by what you do repeatedly. Your accumulated moments.

Small moments of positive choice and action, repeated daily, will slowly lead you in a positive direction. Small moments of negative choice and action, repeated daily, will lead you in a negative direction.

It's really that simple.

So what's the rub? Why do so many struggle with such an easily understood approach to life success?

Why? Because neither choice shows their results immediately.

The good or the bad both take time to manifest. So humans, being the immediate-rewards-driven creatures that we are, tend to make our decisions based on what results we get in the moment. Or said another way, we do what feels good now.

We take the pizza over the salad, the new watch or dress over saving money, the TV over hitting the gym, scrolling through social media over doing valuable work on ourselves.

Small choices that in the moment don't seem all that significant. But, repeated long enough, these seemingly "benign" choices add up, and can easily turn into disaster.

Could eating poorly become a habit? What about eating healthy? Could spending become a habit? What about saving? Could being lazy become a habit? What about being fit? Could avoidance become a habit? What about committing to growth?

Anything repeated long enough—good or bad—can easily become a habit.

The scary part is, the easy, comfortable, immediate-payoff stuff will always have the strongest pull.

So if we want to take control and design the health, happiness, success, and fulfillment plans needed to achieve our goals, we need to become aware of our natural tendencies—AND we need to leverage the power of habits to combat them.

Habits are our leverage points. Our secret weapons. They help us leverage repetition into momentum to fight the good fight, whatever that fight may be.

But, instead of fighting hundreds of daily decisions — decisions that drain us, that catch us at weak moments, that are easily rationalized—instead of trying to muster the willpower to do the right thing and avoid the wrong, we use the power of repetition. Or what I like to call "auto-pilot."

Auto-pilot puts decisions on, well, auto-pilot! We avoid the daily battles of choice and internal negotiating. We build powerful habits—stuff we do no matter what, at this time no matter what, in this way no matter what.

Repeated long enough, these new habits become life patterns that we don't even have to think about. Smart, healthy, wise decisions become simply automatic.

And how cool is that?

Now let's talk about how habits stack. This one can make or break you, and unfortunately, it's often something folks are totally unaware of.

Every positive choice makes the next positive choice easier to do. And every negative choice makes the next negative choice easy to do as well.

Example: If I get up, have a donut and a chocolate milk, you can bet that when lunch rolls around, ordering the nachos and the hot dog will be super easy. It will also make hitting the gym later in the day highly unlikely.

Now, if I get up, and have a fresh smoothie, then come lunch time, ordering the salad and grilled chicken will be a lot easier. And hitting the gym later will be the natural move.

Why? Momentum. For most of us, once we get on the negative side of things, we tend to stay there. Why fight the battle to make a good choice when we've already allowed defeat earlier?

But, if we start on the positive side, it's far easier to maintain it. You've fought and won earlier, so you carry that victory, that momentum, into the next battle.

Becoming hyper-aware of your critical momentum moments is crucial. Learning yourself, and your vulnerabilities—those crossroads moments that will sink the rest of your day—is a game changer.

Once we understand that our lives are simply an accumulation of many small moments, and that by putting the positive moments on auto-pilot we create leverage, and that by stacking these moments we create momentum, we've got a good shot at taking control of our lives and our goals, and making some amazing things happen.

P.S. Habits and discipline are kissing cousins. You won't get anywhere special in life without discipline. The entire goal of this chapter is to help you find a way to cultivate and employ more self-discipline in your life.

Can you simply will it? You can try. Many have, and many have fallen off. Leveraging habits is the best way I know to stoke your self-discipline and give it the fighting chance it deserves.

Action Step

Start a massive habit evaluation process. Decide which habits need to be discarded (those that don't serve you), and which habits need to be created or strengthened (those that do serve you). Be brutally honest with yourself.

Understand that starting and maintaining positive action through the early stages of habit building will almost always be a tough road. Be prepared for the battle!

You will inevitably fall off and struggle as you work to build these habits. Expect it, and get back on the horse.

Find specific times, places, and approaches that allow for certain habits to become built-in to your daily life. Perhaps A.M. workouts are perfect for you ... or maybe it's evening?

Do you study, learn, accomplish more in noisy, public places (a Starbucks perhaps?), or do you do your best in the quiet space of a bedroom?

Do you enjoy a restaurant (or dish) that is healthy? Don't be afraid to eat the same things every day. (I do!)

Most of all, create daily patterns that create consistent, positive progress. Small, consistent steps lead to amazing things.

My Experience

Let's just say I had plenty of habits. Unfortunately, they were almost all the wrong ones.

I was a fast food junkie. (Even after ten years "sober," I've probably still eaten more Taco Bell soft tacos and nachos than any human alive.)

I also regularly consumed gallons of soda, quarts of ice cream, and far too many donuts and cookies ... far too often. (At my worst, I'd grab four donuts and a quart of ice cream every morning for breakfast. Every morning.)

I avoided uncomfortable encounters, uncomfortable conversations, and uncomfortable work in favor of the easy stuff. Avoidance and procrastination were gold medal events for me.

I spent money (whenever I **DID** manage to get a little) on extravagant things that made me feel good in the moment and cost me dearly in every other aspect of life.

I focused on fun and feeling good, rather than doing the hard work to build a quality life. I also had no problem with irresponsible, integrity-free behavior.

I fought dramatic weight fluctuations. I got into all kinds of trouble because I wouldn't handle things until they blew up. I had massive financial, credit, and life security issues. I floated through life, squandering my potential, my responsibilities, and even hurting people.

These were all habits. Stuff I'd done for so long that I didn't even think to examine them. That's the power of habit.

That should be terrifying. Looking back and seeing how easily I lived that way, it sure is for me.

And as we talked about earlier in the chapter, all these habits were stacking—both individually and collectively.

Meaning, they individually green-lighted more of the same behaviors, and they collectively green-lighted the overall sense of "why bother trying to change any of it?" It all worked together to create a feeling of overwhelm and acceptance.

So what intervened? Ah, I'm so glad you asked.

What changed is the topic we started the book off with: Influences.

New influences started showing me not just new skills and mindset shifts, but, as I mentioned earlier, they also caused me to raise my bar for acceptable behavior in general.

Of course, pain was also involved. I hated the way I felt—physically, mentally, emotionally. So it was perfect timing. A collision of pain and answers.

I started with a few things. I started studying personal development books first thing in the morning, and while I ate lunch. I listened to audiobooks and programs in the car. I did this for at least two hours a day, but usually more.

I started walking my dogs 90 minutes in the morning, after studying, and another 45 minutes at night ... religiously.

Without knowing it, I was starting to stack some habits. I was starting my day with the right brain work and the right body work.

That created some momentum.

From there, getting back into working out was a natural move. And that led to wanting to eat better too. I ended up losing 30 pounds over the next year.

With my new influences constantly nipping at my heels, I became more conscious about my finances, my taxes, my credit, and my spending. I also started diving into the work that wasn't easy. Work for my newly-birthed business. Work on my relationship, communication, and emotional skills.

Pretty soon, I had a host of new habits. I realized that I thrived on the repetition and that through this repetition, I could slowly build great things ... internally and externally.

Now, after years of embedding these habits, I feel strange and incomplete if I skip them. The joys of immediate gratification were replaced with the joys of long-term gratification, and long-term self-respect and health.

I won't say it's always easy, and I won't say I'm always perfect—I'm far from it. But once you get a taste of what's possible, and you practice it long enough for it to become a part of you, it sure gets a lot easier.

5 Action:
The Fuel

"Action expresses priorities." — **Mahatma Gandhi**

Doing. It's the hard part, and it's the scary part.

The hard part: Let's face it, we're all lazy. Come on, tell the truth. I know I am. Humans, by nature, are always on the lookout for comfort and ease. It's hardwired. So that's just always going to be there.

Our laziness tells us to stay in bed a little longer, scroll through Facebook a few more minutes, watch just one more show, or that we can get to that tomorrow.

They all sound good, don't they?

The scary part: Doing exposes us. Once we take action, we show the world our hopes, our beliefs, our dreams. We also expose ourselves to reality. Taking action reveals whether something actually works or not.

Our protective self says, "What if they laugh, what if I'm wrong, what if it fails, what if I'm not good enough?"

These all sound pretty bad, don't they?

Between the hard part of fighting laziness and the scary part of exposing ourselves, it's amazing we do anything at all!

But as hard and scary as it might be, here's the problem: Nothing happens without it.

The healthy body, the valuable mind, the relationship with your family and friends, the career, the goals, the dreams.

It's only action that brings any of them to you.

If you want any of the good stuff that life has to offer, you'll have to make yourself intimately comfortable with action ... and often, discomfort.

This means doing things you don't want to do, pushing on when you want to stop, and risking when you'd rather hide. It means sharing instead of shutting down, working on yourself when you'd rather tune-out, and trying again even after you've failed (again).

It often means working harder than those around you, looking for answers more deeply than those around you, and connecting ideas better than those around you.

Life rewards effort, sacrifice, and risk. It's really that simple. The more you're willing to put on the table, the more rewards come your way.

And that's the beauty of it.

There's no gaming the system. There's no crafty worka-rounds. There's no "working smarter" that supersedes it. No genius, talent, or imagination that replaces it. There are no shortcuts available—to anyone.

It's a simple, clear, fair transaction. One that puts anyone willing to do the work in a position to win.

This is where we turn the mental into the physical. Where dreams go from vision to reality.

The miracle of creation occurs here.

You see it, you decide on it, you take action towards it every day, and boom(!), something that once was fantasy is now reality.

All through action.

How much action? How much work? How much risk? That all depends on you and the size of your goals, dreams, and aspirations.

The more you want from life, the more you have to give to it. The more you give, the more you get.

So it's really all up to you. You get to choose. You either adjust your action, or you adjust your dreams.

Action Step

Check in with yourself often. Are you doing all that you could be doing to achieve your goals and improve your life? Do your actions equal your dreams and desires?

This reality check habit can help keep you straight with yourself. If you can start every day with a truly honest "action evaluation," you'll be far more likely to do what you need to.

Just start. Don't wait for things to be perfect or all set. They will never be. Just get going. You'll get plenty of feedback once you get started. You can tweak, improve, and adjust as you go.

Over-planning and perfectionism are behaviors people commonly use to avoid doing what they should. Just start!

Also, check in with **WHAT** you're doing. Is it just activity (comfortable busy-ness), or is it valuable (and perhaps scary) action moving you closer to your goals? This is another common distraction and avoidance trap people fall into.

Always do more than you are paid for or than is expected from you. Nothing moves you along faster towards success than giving more value than you ask in return.

My Experience

I was a genius. I had a gift for avoidance, procrastination, and distraction that some would call world-class. I could rationalize and fool myself into doing just about anything, as long as it was comfy and avoided anything unpleasant.

If there was something I had to do that wasn't fun and novel, and a big chunk of time to do it in, you can bet that I would screw around until I'd whittled that big chunk into a little one.

That was my game. Avoid the uncomfortable as long as possible, and then, when time was super tight, when I couldn't avoid it any longer, I'd jump in, stressed and overwhelmed, and do a crappy rush job.

And that's with the stuff I **HAD** to do ...

This doesn't even get into all the stuff I **SHOULD** have been doing! I should have been working on, oh, about a million other aspects of my life that were a mess. But nope, I was comfy just being comfy.

This was the perfect plan for a half-assed life, but a terrible plan for a great one.

As I studied those who were doing great things, I started to see some themes. Discipline, focus, structure, doing the uncomfortable, and a ton of just hard work.

Uh-oh.

I had to retrain myself. If I was ever going to make anything special happen, I had to learn to do the things I didn't want to do. The hard, the unpleasant, the mundane. And I had to learn to cut out all the avoidant, procrastination stuff that was derailing me.

I had to get disciplined, and fast.

I surrounded myself with influences that continuously pushed me to not only work harder but to view work differently.

I realized I could reprogram myself to view work (even the boring, uncomfortable stuff) as something "sexy" and cool. Instead of resisting and avoiding, I could get excited and take pride in the sacrifice and discipline—knowing these moments of action were moving me forward.

Reframing the work in this way, and learning to see it as the gateway to closing the gap between where I was and where I wanted to be, and who I was and who I wanted to be, gave everything I was doing a totally different feeling.

Once I made that shift, my avoidant, procrastination-rich habits began to fade. Crazily enough, I became known as a hard worker!

I had developed a new mindset. A mindset where long hours and tough, challenging work had not only become the norm, it was something I welcomed.

6 Mindset and Attitude: The Magnet

"A positive attitude causes a chain reaction of positive thoughts, events, and outcomes. It is a catalyst, and it sparks extraordinary results." — **Wade Boggs**

One of the trickiest and easiest traps to fall victim to is ... you. Or, shall I say, your mindset and attitude.

Could your mental state be creating obstacles and barriers to your happiness and success?

You bet.

Could you be totally unaware of your part in creating this reality?

Yep.

So many go through life feeling they've been done dirty. That opportunities and "luck" happen to other folks. That no matter how hard they try, they're always getting overlooked, taken advantage of, or just plain screwed.

They blame life, and they blame others. But the only person consistently on the scene when everything goes wrong is them.

They can't figure out why they seem to attract negative people and negative situations, and why the "good stuff" and the "good ones" always seem to elude them.

But the why is actually pretty simple.

Mindset and attitude act like a magnet. They can attract or repel, all depending on who you are and what you share.

If life has seemed like a never-ending uphill battle, this is an excellent point for self-examination. You've likely been sabotaging yourself without even knowing it. You've been a magnet, just not the kind you've wanted to be.

But it doesn't have to be a life sentence.

By deciding to change what you share with the world—kindness, generosity, understanding, optimism, joy, etc.—you can attract entirely different types of people to you.

And through these different people, new and previously unavailable opportunities and connections will begin to show up.

Opportunities and connections that can help build your dreams, achieve your goals, and create fulfilling and rewarding relationships.

Of course, the opposite is also true. If you're going through life with a toxic, negative, gossiping, whining, complaining, victim-y attitude and mindset, you will repel these quality people and all the opportunities they may have to offer.

Doors will close that you never even knew were there. Opportunities will gravitate to someone else. Your "string of bad luck" will continue.

Those who exist in a negative state create a self-fulfilling prophecy. They think negatively, and life gives them negativity back. And the more life confirms their negative beliefs, the more negative these people become.

Does this mean you have to put on a happy face and not be real? No, of course not. Don't confuse positivity with shallow or phony.

What this does mean is that you make a conscious effort (especially when things are hard) to look for the upside, to practice gratitude, to see possibility rather than limitation. To work towards solutions rather than friction, to search for the good instead of the bad in others.

It means doing the hard, emotional work to ensure you don't share crappy, negative baggage unconsciously. Baggage that can easily keep the best of what life has to offer just out of reach.

If you'll work your butt off to create and sustain a positive attitude and mindset, you'll become that magnet for good that you've always wanted to be. Good people and good things will "mysteriously" start to show up more regularly in your life. Your "luck" will get a dramatic overhaul.

And those roadblocks, potholes, and closed doors? You'll start to see a whole lot less of them.

Action Step

Become highly tuned-in to your attitude and mindset. Are you thinking negative thoughts about yourself or others? Do you expect things to go wrong? Do you believe that life has it out for you? Are you always expecting the other shoe to drop?

Ask yourself these questions—and answer honestly. Awareness is the first step to change.

Also, check in with what it's like to be around both positive and negative people. How do their different attitudes affect you? How do you feel? Attracted or repelled? Do you want to spend more time with them or less?

A great exercise is what I call the "opposite exercise." Any time you find yourself sliding into a judgmental, annoyed, righteous, or victim-y space, practice doing the opposite.

Say someone annoys you, and you find yourself going to that toxic spot. Stop, and send the person a thought of love. Literally say in your mind, "I love you" or "I hope you're okay." Dig down deep to find empathy. Imagine what experiences might have led them to where they are and how they're behaving.

Let's say you're feeling righteous and struggling to find understanding for another. Do a quick mental scan on all the terrible choices and behaviors you regret. Imagine all the times you've been ashamed of yourself. Does that make finding understanding any easier?

Or, let's say you're feeling victimized and "unlucky." Do a reality check on all you have to be grateful for in your life. Imagine someone who's truly struggling—perhaps someone with a terminal disease or someone who is homeless. Do some comparing. Still feeling unlucky?

Doing the opposite exercise totally undermines the nasty outlook you were falling into. It changes toxic feelings to kindness, judgment to empathy, and will eventually re-pattern the way you see others—and yourself.

My Experience

Whew. Here's where things get a little ugly. Let's just say my mindset and attitude weren't exactly going to win me any awards. I was bitter, blaming, pissed off, and certain I'd gotten a raw deal—from everyone and everything.

In an effort to bolster my lack of self-esteem and lack of self-love, I indulged in a full-time campaign of working to tear everyone else down.

I was happy to gossip, criticize, judge, belittle, and marginalize. All in an effort to try to feel better about myself.

This toxic state created mountains of self-loathing on top of the mountains I was already struggling with. You can't think crappy thoughts about others and not feel crappy about yourself.

But I was hurt and angry and felt the world owed me considerably. So that's how I carried myself, and that's what I shared.

Knowing what I know now, it's not surprising that the world was more than happy to send all that toxic stuff right back at me.

We always get what we focus on, and boy, was I focused on the wrong stuff. So I got lots of it. Crappy jobs, crappy relationships, crappy breaks, crappy feelings about myself.

Of course, it wasn't life's problem. It was mine.

Life simply gives you back what you put out. You get what you are, what you believe, and what you share.

I had to work overtime on this one to make even a little progress. I had toxicity oozing from me consciously and unconsciously. It was a deeply embedded mental habit pattern.

I worked hard to become aware of all my thoughts, and any time the ugly stuff came up, I played the opposite game. I saw a therapist weekly, who helped me connect and process pieces I wasn't able to on my own. I kept my new influences front and center to ensure I stayed on track with who I wanted to become.

Slowly, I began to view the world and myself differently. I managed to find more understanding, gratitude, joy, kindness, and generosity.

Amazingly, I was actually becoming someone I felt good about. Someone I was proud of.

And that's when a life of change and opportunity began showing up on the regular.

When my mindset changed, so did everything else.

7 Prosperity Consciousness:
What You Believe is What You Get

> "*Prosperity is a way of living and thinking, and not just having money or things. Poverty is a way of living and thinking, and not just a lack of money or things.*" — **Eric Butterworth**

I call this one the "life assassin." Why? Because more than any of the other principles here, this one seems to quietly, and without the awareness of the victim, undermine and destroy our human potential.

It doesn't require you to be lazy, irresponsible, or a bad person.

It just requires you to not understand it.

In fact, most of those who fall victim to it are hard-working, responsible, character-rich folks.

So how do good, hard working people end up with far smaller, far less impactful lives? Why do they struggle with money, with dreaming bigger, with achieving all they're capable of?

I'll tell you how.

Your true subconscious feelings, programmed into you by your family, friends, and society, about money, wealth, success, and yourself, will determine what you go after, what you keep, and what you become.

If you feel that money, or the desire for it, makes you greedy, or will take from someone else, you will struggle.

If you feel that rich or successful people got there by doing other folks dirty, you will struggle.

If you were told over and over by your parents (or society) to be practical and safe and to not shoot too high, you will struggle.

If you feel unworthy or ashamed of who you are and things you've experienced or done, you will struggle.

Why the struggle? Simple. You won't go after what you don't feel good about.

If you think going after money is bad, you won't go after it. If you think rich people are bad, you won't become one of them.

If you think aiming too high makes you too ambitious, you'll make sure your aim is nice and reasonable.

If you feel bad about who you are, you'll never feel deserving of good and will avoid going after it.

And if by some strange twist you do end up with a lucky break—financially, romantically, or career-wise—you'll subconsciously sabotage that luck. You'll bring yourself back to your comfort zone—or your "deserve" zone.

We all get programming messages when we're kids from family and society about money, wealth, ambition, and ourselves. It gets in there early and infects our beliefs, and subsequently our actions. (Remember that whole influence thing?)

Most of us don't even know we're infected and being controlled by these beliefs. But we are.

So what do we do to take back control of our lives? How do we get a handle on this early-installed program that's running our thoughts and decisions—often without us even knowing?

Becoming self-aware is the first step. You've got to acknowledge that this programming exists and that it affects your choices, decisions, and behaviors. Then, you've got to do a major examination. You've got to dive deeply and honestly into your early programming.

Once you find ground zero—your current beliefs—then you can go to work on replacing those that don't serve you.

If we find we have money issues, we need to retrain ourselves to see money as something positive. Something that is the physical representation of value given. Something that creates options, freedom, and security. Something that can be used to create amazing good in the world.

If we find we have ambition issues, we need to retrain ourselves to see that developing our potential is our greatest responsibility to ourselves and the world. We need to understand that **NOT** reaching as high as we can and **NOT** exploring all we have to offer is the greatest crime we can commit.

If we have personal worthiness issues, we need to retrain ourselves to see ourselves as being worthy of joy, happiness, fulfillment, love, and success. We need to work through whatever trauma, pain, and programming has convinced us we deserve less or are worth less.

Can you see how prosperity consciousness—which is simply your beliefs about prosperity and yourself—could be the silent killer of dreams, goals, and happiness?

Can you see how you could **THINK** you're going full-tilt towards your best, but have this insidious program running in the back of your mind, constantly keeping you from achieving it?

Because this is typically an early, intimate, and socially-comprehensive embedding of beliefs, it can be one of the hardest to get a healthy handle on. It's easy for it to become a mental blind spot.

Early beliefs and programming feel like they are us. But they aren't. They're simply someone else's programming and beliefs passed on to us—often without them even knowing they're doing it.

It's our job to recover ourselves, to rebuild ourselves. We have to wipe the slate clean, and then draw up new, healthy beliefs. Beliefs built on our experience and conclusions, not others'.

Action Step

Practice seeing people with greater success as having created more value, solved bigger problems, worked harder than you, been more creative than you, and helped more people than you.

Instead of judging or criticizing those with more, mentally salute them for what they've achieved. Focus on individuals that inspire you with their generosity and integrity.

DO NOT focus on those who you THINK might have done things the "wrong" way. This will only slow your progress. (You can find confirmation bias in either direction. Choose your focus wisely.)

Work to see those with abundance in a positive fashion. It will help break you out of your toxic mindset about money, success, and the people who have it, which will free you up to attract these things into your own life.

Also, take some serious time to check in with any negative money, wealth, and prosperity messages you might have received over your life (especially in childhood). These messages are everywhere. Uncovering and examining them is crucial to your development.

Explore your true feelings about yourself. Do you truly feel you deserve the best from life? Do you struggle with shame and negative self-image? These feelings may need deep work. If so, find a professional and get help.

Trying to attain success and happiness without first addressing these core emotional issues leads to more unhappiness and failure.

My Experience

I didn't even know this was a thing! I assumed we all wanted to be happy, successful, have lots of money, and that we were all comfy with that—including me. Boy, was I mistaken.

After this realization, I decided to take a look at my early messages about money and success...and life. Yikes!

As a child of early divorce, I basically had two families.

I realized my mom's side of the family had always viewed rich folks suspiciously. There wasn't much direct trash talking, just more of an undertone of wariness and mistrust. But I definitely felt the us-versus-them vibe.

I also realized that talking about money, wealth, success, potential, or anything to do with truly large goals was something we'd never done. It just wasn't part of our conversation.

On my dad's side, there were many of the same messages and omissions, but there was also an added element. My dad had always struggled terribly with money. Food stamps, welfare, eviction notices, and the constant struggle to get by was ever-present.

I realized that a deep-seated part of me believed that I could never do better than my dad. I thought, "Who am I to ever think I could do better than my own father?"

So I had the perfect "prosperity-lack" cocktail. Plenty of negative messages about money, success, and a bigger life, and zero positive messages.

I was honestly stunned when I did this work. I had had no idea what kind of programming I was working from. I had assumed that we all (myself included) naturally wanted the best, the most, the greatest from life. I hadn't realized that our programming, or lack thereof, could be derailing us so deeply.

This doesn't even touch on all the societal messages I received about money, the wealthy, and the successful. Take a close look at most stories in all forms of media (cartoons, books, movies—with perhaps hip-hop being one of the few exceptions), and you'll almost always find a rich villain and a poor hero.

One other crucial element in all this was my emotional state. Coming from what I shared in the introduction of the book, there were mountains of emotional roadblocks and pitfalls to resolve.

Self-esteem and self-love were in short supply. Self-loathing and shame were running the show.

So I had lots of work to do. But I was actually immensely relieved to find out that there was a cause behind so much of the struggle. Once you know, you can go! Once you understand the problem, you can go about fixing it.

And so I did.

I went to work replacing my early messages with new messages (and influences).

I followed and studied folks who had done great things and created great wealth. I worked hard to re-program myself about what I could do and become.

I practiced all the exercises I listed in the "Action Step" above. (Those actions came directly from me and my journey to turn things around.)

I also saw a therapist for many, many years (and still do on occasion). We worked through years of baggage to help clear the path for a happier, healthier, more prosperous life.

And I studied as many books as I could to help work through my issues.

Slowly, with lots of work, things began to shift—just a little. And then a little more. And then a lot more!

Within a few years, I was operating from a very different set of beliefs. I was dreaming big, I was feeling worthy, and I was taking action on all of it.

Although it sounds a bit trite and boastful, I don't intend it that way, but it is my truth. Within a few years, I had left the valet world. I had started what would be the first of several businesses. Life began to shift in some fairly monumental ways.

I had worked hard to reprogram myself, untangle myself, heal myself. And the fruits of that work were starting to pay off.

P.S. I also want to clarify that my mom's side of the family showed me what hard work, integrity, responsibility, and sacrifice looked like. I thank them deeply for all they did and still do.

8 Embracing Failure: The Unexpected Teacher

> *"If failure is not an option, then neither is success."*
> — Seth Godin

Failure gets a bad rap. It needs a re-frame. A make-over.

Somehow, the thing that teaches, informs, guides, corrects, and enlightens us best has become this personal and social bogeyman, to be avoided at all costs.

Over and over we're taught, either directly or through the reactions of those around us, that failing, struggling, and messing up are synonymous with actually being a failure.

It becomes a scarlet letter about our value that we allow others to pin on us and that we pin on ourselves as well.

When messing something up becomes the same as being a mess-up, you can see how quickly human beings would curtail their vulnerability, creativity, and willingness to risk.

This is why our perspective on failure is in such desperate need of an overhaul. Because when humans equate failing with being a failure, we all lose.

People don't speak up. People don't take chances. People don't try things, or build things, or dream things.

Imagine just about everything you enjoy and use in life. Your car, your smartphone, your house, the restaurant down the street, the airplane you fly in, the medicine that keeps you healthy, your favorite band or book or movie or TV show.

Imagine if the people behind all these things had been too afraid to take a chance? Too afraid to be made fun of? Too afraid to fail?

All that amazing stuff—poof! Gone. Just like that. And why? Not for lack of ability or talent, but simply due to the fear of failing.

Can you see why we need a make-over?

In the big picture, re-framing failure is crucial to our quality of life and the advancement of humanity. It's how we progress.

But let's take a step back. Let's define this beast.

What is failure? I mean really, what is it?

It's simply information. Information that informs you whether something you're doing is working or not. Whether you're on the right track or not. Whether you need to re-tweak, rethink, redo, or not.

Once you remove all the social and personal pressures associated with it, you can see failure for what it is. It's not a value judgment about you and your personal worth. It's just feedback.

And feedback sounds pretty good. It's how we learn and improve and do amazing things.

It helps you get back on course when you've strayed. It helps you revamp the thing that just isn't clicking. It alerts you to problems and issues that need addressing.

Once we re-frame failure as a wise and direct teacher, we can take the feedback for what it is. We can welcome the information, make the necessary adjustments, and we can move forward.

Can it hurt? Sure. Should it hurt? Probably. Pain is a powerful teacher and usually the necessary wingman of failure.

Oftentimes it's only pain that has enough behind it to push us to make uncomfortable choices and changes.

But the pain of messing up, and the pain of being a mess-up always need to be clearly differentiated.

You aren't a mistake, you make mistakes, and missing that distinction can be catastrophic. It can be the difference between a vibrant, bold life, and a quiet, safe one.

Your mistakes mean you're in the game. They mean you're trying. They mean you're risking. And for that, you need to applaud yourself. It puts you in the tiny minority of those willing to put themselves out there, and say, "Hey world, here ya go! What do you think?"

The truth is, we need a lot more folks willing to risk. We need you to stand up and share your gifts. Even if the first few versions of those gifts might need a bit of tweaking. (It's not supposed to work right out of the box!)

Yes, mistakes might sting a little, or they might feel world-ending, but those experiences of discomfort, regardless of intensity, will never come close to the dark, lasting pain of knowing you could have been and done more ... and didn't.

Action Step

Make a concerted effort to stand back and evaluate your relationship with failure. What does failure mean to you? What do you feel when you imagine failing? Who do you see judging you if you fail?

Have you bought in to the failing-equals-failure message? Do you equate mistakes with your personal value? Does failing make you feel worthless?

Check in with your family's programming about failing. Were there messages that only success and accomplishment earned love and attention? Were there messages that you were worthless, flawed, or unworthy of love?

Work hard to re-frame failing as the proof that you're trying. If you can start to take pride in the process of trying, risking, and learning—regardless of outcome—you've moved to a higher mental place.

Pick out something you've wanted to do, but were afraid to start (or finish) and go after it. Now. Prove to yourself you can break old patterns of fear, and build on it.

Get into the habit of trying, risking, and saying yes to new adventures and possibilities. Practice saying yes to life, even when it scares you. The fear usually means it's something you need to explore and learn from.

My Experience, Part 1

I make mistakes daily. Mistakes in my business, mistakes in my time management, mistakes in my spending, mistakes in my communication and relationships. And I'll be honest; I hate each one of them. I hate seeing my gaps. But, each of these mistakes teaches me. They expand me and force me to grow. They make me better.

Some of these mistakes are little reminders, and some are enormous life changers. They all hurt, and that hurt helps to push me to look for better ways to handle things next time. Without the hurt, there's no motivation for change.

I also understand I'm always going to be growing and learning—closing the gap—and thus, making mistakes. So I work hard to be as easy on myself when I mess up as I am hard on myself to be better. There's always that push and pull.

Another fascinating thing I've noticed is that whatever I'm most afraid of, most worried about, most trying to avoid, always ends up being my biggest breakthrough.

Why? Because if the fear is so big, it's an excellent indicator that there's something major I need to face and grow through.

We're never afraid of the stuff we're good at or prepared for. Fear lives in our gaps. I know the more I'm avoiding or afraid of something, the more crucial it is for me to tackle it.

Once I've finally faced it and worked through it, I always realize there's been an enormous upside of growth—growth that would have never occurred had I stayed static and "safe."

I've also realized the only way to find out what works and what doesn't is to simply try it. There's no way to figure out if something is good or if it works by sitting on it.

Fence-sitting (being too afraid to make a decision or take a chance) is the least effective and most painful way to find out anything. Trust me; I've sat on far too many fences of my own.

You have to make a move to get the feedback, and the only feedback fence-sitting gives is anxiety.

So it's far better to jump off, commit to a choice, and actually find out if it works or not. You can always change your mind and make a new choice. (A better one now that you have more information.) But without actually trying it, you will never know 100% what's right.

These days, I do a lot less fence-sitting, a lot less avoiding, and a lot more chance-taking. I know I'll always make mistakes, but I also know that each mistake pushes me a little farther ahead, and closes that gap just a little more.

My Experience, Part 2

Growing up in super-critical family environments, I developed an intense fear of failing. The messaging was this: Failing or messing up was directly equated with my personal worth.

Rather than failure being about an event or behavior, it became about who I was. That made failure something to be pretty terrified of.

It brought on intense self-consciousness, crippling shyness, and mountains of self-doubt.

To preserve myself, I worked on becoming invisible. I hid in my classes and at school in general. I didn't talk to others because I never trusted myself to know what to say. I was always terrified I'd be found out as being stupid or uncool or unacceptable.

This continued through school and adulthood. I struggled in social settings, always unsure and uneasy, and I kept to myself more and more.

I developed intense social and performance anxiety, which crept into everything. It would cause me to mentally and physically freeze. Mini panic attacks became common in my life.

I got used to operating at about 50% of who I was. Always fighting anxiety, the true me was rarely available.

Self-worth issues kept the anxiety high and the risking low. I took whatever jobs, friends, and romantic relationships that came my way. I didn't have the self-esteem to expect or ask for anything more.

This meant that instead of creating a healthy, bold, challenging, and fulfilling life, I took whatever I got. And what I got was exactly what you get when things are broken: unhealthy, toxic, safe, stagnant stuff.

It wasn't until I started to do my work—therapy, self-help books, self-analysis, etc.—that things started to shift.

Little by little, I began to rebuild myself. I gained tools and understanding about myself and others that I'd been missing most of my life.

I started to lighten up, to see actions and choices and opinions I expressed as being non-life-threatening. I took bigger and bolder steps. I started asking more from life.

I learned that I wasn't the person that all those pro-grammed messages told me I was.

I learned that messing up didn't make me a mess-up.

I also learned that sometimes it's simply not about you.

I'd be lying if I said it was easy or that I don't still struggle with some of this stuff. But what I've managed to do with all the failure baggage and worthiness baggage, is pretty cool. It makes me proud.

It's proof that even if we come from challenging situations, even if we were taught to equate failing with being a failure, even if we've been directly told we were failures, we can all still fight our way though, and share our gifts.

9 Growth: The Only Constant

> *"Learning is the beginning of wealth. Learning is the beginning of health. Learning is the beginning of spirituality. Searching and learning is where the miracle process all begins."*
> —Jim Rohn

So how do we close this gap? How do we continually move towards our better selves? It's actually pretty simple.

We make growth—learning, developing, improving—a consistent, daily part of who and what we are. We commit to educating ourselves, in all capacities.

Remember, the gap is simply the space between the current you and the potential you. You close that space through knowledge, insight, and expanding who you are.

The current you, no matter how evolved, has gaps and limits that affect the quality of your life, in every aspect.

Your communication, your problem solving, your financial abilities, your emotional depth, your health, your career skills, your happiness, and on and on.

All these skills and many others are developed and cultivated through the work of searching, studying, and applying—or not.

Building your best life—a life where the current you and your potential you are in a constant state of moving towards each other—requires lifelong commitment to being a constant student.

This means studying books, audio, videos, movies, family, friends, co-workers, and society in general.

Everyone has something to teach us, so if we're smart, we'll be studying—well, everyone! Some will teach you what to do, and some will teach you what not to do.

Your job is to pull the best information from everywhere and everyone, regardless of where you find them. If you're really looking, you'll be amazed at how many teachers you'll find in everyday life, doing everyday things. Often, it's the gas station clerk or the stranger that holds the door open for us that reminds us about kindness and generosity.

Along with your "everyday" teachers, you should assemble your collection of more "formal" teachers or mentors. These are people (real or virtual) who exude qualities, traits, and skills that you admire. People you want to borrow from and emulate. The goal being that you steal a bit of their greatness and make it your own.

By building the habit and mindset of the "forever student"—someone who is always thirsty for more knowledge and understanding—you will tap into what famed speaker Jim Rohn calls "the miracle process."

The miracle process is simply being in a constant state of growth. You're always looking, examining, analyzing, expanding, deepening.

This one critical distinction in thought and outlook on life can be the difference between finding your greatness or simply getting by.

All the greatest minds, the wisest of the wise—not to mention the happiest, most centered, and most successful people—are in a constant state of change and growth.

They're never just sitting still mentally. They're always challenging themselves. Pushing. Searching. Looking in the cracks for pearls of wisdom they might have missed, and opportunities to expand their minds and beliefs and understanding.

These folks are excited about being in this state. Growth becomes who they are. It becomes a habit and something they crave.

Every day is another opportunity for them to be a little better than yesterday. And they relish that challenge. They know they're closing the gap a little more.

Unfortunately, there's the flip side of this mindset as well. Take a look around at those you know who are struggling and ask yourself: "How much time do these folks spend daily on self-improvement? How hard are they working on themselves?"

This points out how essential learning, growing, and improving are to not just life success, but also happiness in general.

Those focused on just getting by, taking the easy path, wasting time, zoning out with TV or video games or gossip, will never be the ones enjoying the happy, prosperous, challenging lives they could be.

They might be getting by, but they aren't closing the gap. They aren't inching closer to their greatness.

So, could the differentiator between the haves and the have-nots, the happy and the unhappy, the prosperous and the unprosperous, the fulfilled and the unfulfilled, come down to something as simple as cultivating a mindset of daily growth?

100%.

It's amazing that something so profound and so important is that simple. Just a shift in perspective and action. Nothing cosmic, nothing otherworldly. Simple, tangible, and most of all, doable.

All the information you need to build an exceptional life is just sitting there, waiting for you!

Yes, you have to dig for it. Yes, you have to sift through it. And yes, you have to absorb and apply it. But if that's the price of a great life, isn't that a steal?

Action Step

Make a serious commitment to start a personal library of transformational books, audio, and videos. Your single best investment will be the time and money you invest in your own personal growth.

Set aside a chunk of non-negotiable time every day to study. (Remember the power of habits! This consistency is what makes this practice powerful.) It creates momentum and reinforces the growth mindset daily.

Listen to audiobooks or podcasts in your car, or while you're showering or working out. Read and watch videos (and take notes!) when your mind is quiet and able to focus. Find that special study time and the locations that work best for you.

Search out the teachers and concepts that speak most directly to you. This is a very personal process. When you find something or someone you like, dive in! But remember to seek out other voices and perspectives to keep you as multi-dimensional and balanced as possible.

I personally have a morning study routine of at least an hour before getting out of bed (but it's usually more), and another hour of videos or podcasts while at the gym. Full disclosure: when I started this process, I spent about four hours a day studying.

My Experience

This is an interesting one for me. While I've always been curious, searching, and learning, I've almost always been curious, searching, and learning about the wrong things.

I didn't know there was something more important to learn about—namely, myself, life, and how to be a more valuable member of this world.

I didn't know that mastering life as much as possible was a far better (and more fulfilling) way to spend my time than watching TV, hanging out, reading magazines, or listening to talk radio.

The concept of closing the gap between who I was and who I could be wasn't even on my radar. I was just "doing time."

Luckily, I found several mentors who turned the lights on for me. I realized I had been wasting my time and my life.

I started dedicating a significant portion of every day to the study of life-mastery and self-mastery. I challenged my emotions and my intellect. I worked on critical thinking and honest self-evaluation.

Through hundreds of books, videos, and audios, along with copious note-taking and analysis, I made huge strides.

I blew apart old, limiting beliefs, and I replaced them with new, empowering ones. I developed entirely new perspectives and views on life, priorities, and possibilities.

I can, without question, point to this daily study routine as THE cause for all the positive changes I underwent in my life. This single practice began what was to be a complete overhaul of the old me into the new me.

But just so we're clear, none of this happened overnight. There was no seamless ascent. No way. I was far too much of a mess for that kind of easy ride. I was working hard, no doubt, but I had years and years of negative beliefs and programming and habits to untangle.

At times it was frustrating. Once I saw all that was out there and in here, and how much time I had wasted, I wanted it. I wanted it now. But it took time—lots of it.

But just being on the path felt amazing. Yes, I was a million miles from where I wanted to be, but after so many years of being lost, finally connecting to what I believed was the meaning of life—working towards becoming my best self—I was far more elated than frustrated.

And even if things were moving more slowly than I wanted, my life began to morph dramatically. I was building a new me, and everything in my outside world was beginning to reflect the changes of my inside world.

I had become a committed, forever student, and was quickly learning that there was no finish line. It was just this ongoing journey, this forever process.

But I also knew it wasn't forever. There was a clock running. There was only so much time I was going to have, to see who and what I could become, and who and what I could impact, before that clock stopped.

And that's why I still study so hard today.

10 Persistence: Beyond Survival

> *"Sometimes life knocks you on your ass ... get up, get up, get up!!! Happiness is not the absence of problems, it's the ability to deal with them."* — **Steve Maraboli**

PART ONE

Let me share a little secret. We all struggle. I don't care how "together" things look on the outside, and I don't care how elevated their status may appear, everyone struggles. Everyone.

The ability we have to cultivate and control what others perceive ends up running a serious game on all of us.

We see all these folks we admire—famous, successful, and even just "normal" people, seemingly kicking life's butt. But, what you don't see, and what most work extremely hard to conceal, is the mess.

Ah, the mess. It comes in all sorts of packages and presentations, but trust me, no one's dodging it.

What is the mess? Family problems, relationship problems, financial problems, health problems, emotional problems, business and career problems … and a million others.

The whole setup of life is simply a series of problems that we have to find our way through.

Sounds like a tough setup, but that's the setup.

Rather than resist it, avoid it, or be upset by it, it's better to just acknowledge the rules of the game and get on with it.

And know you're not alone.

Not that it makes solving the actual problems easier. The challenges and obstacles you'll face will still be there. But understand that this boat we're in is full of others all muddling through, screwing up, stressing out, and freaking out. That should help make the trip a little more bearable, a little less lonely, and far from unique to just you.

Because the truth is, anyone you know is battling. They're battling their past, they're battling their present, and they're battling their future.

You might not see it all. But trust me, it's all going down.

And that, in so many ways, is the true magnificence of the human animal—our ability to persist and push on.

We're built, programmed, and engineered to keep moving forward, even in the face of seemingly insurmountable situations. Our survival drive, problem solving, and coping abilities are wondrous.

PART TWO

But is that all we're built for? Are we designed to just get by? Are we engineered to just survive the challenges of life?

So many, with so much to offer, hit a personal wall. They hit a space where they realize that the more they reach for, the harder things get.

So—rather than push themselves and use this amazing machine designed to push boundaries, create the uncreated, and deliver dreams—they let up. They choose comfort and ease over potential and greatness.

And to be honest, they're right. It IS easier to let up. It IS more comfortable to coast. Pushing is hard. Risking is hard. Reaching is hard.

And knowing all that, it brings us to a decision point: What do we choose to do with this one life?

Do we take this machine, built for greatness—a machine with a definite expiration date—and use it to its fullest, knowing it will be a harder, but far more fulfilling journey? Or do we let up, allowing our best to escape us, and choose an easier, but ultimately, far less fulfilling experience?

This may be the most important question you'll ever ask yourself.

And this is why I placed *Influences* as the first chapter. If folks don't have the right support, the right direction, and the right influences pushing them forward, demanding their best, and encouraging them on, it's easy to let up and let go. Especially when things get rough.

For many without the right push, and without the understanding that it's supposed to be hard, they decide that navigating regular life is hard enough.

So going for greatness and choosing the harder path is something that's not even on the menu. Why go for greatness when regular life is already this hard?

But were you built for regular? Were you built to just get by?

If you really search yourself, if you really dig past the regular-ness that most of society has come to accept as "life," I think the answer is pretty obvious.

You weren't built for either of the above. You were built to reach for your best, and you know it. It's the discomfort, not the greatness, that you're hiding from.

So what does all this have to do with persistence?

I like to think of persistence as having two distinct parts.

The first is the one we're all familiar with: survival. Getting by. This one is hardwired into us. We don't have to work for this one.

No matter how bad things get, our internal program tells us to keep pushing forward. Find food, find shelter, find a mate. Survive.

It also tells us—after we've got the survival thing down—to find comfort. Find a job that feels comfortable, find a place to live that feels comfortable, make enough money to be safe and prepared, and … comfortable.

That's the basic, cruise-control persistence. It's based on comfort and getting by with the least amount of struggle. It's not a persistence of challenges, dreams, and striving. It's just genetics.

But there's another persistence. This one isn't genetically built in. This one is mentally built up.

This is the persistence of a much smaller group. A group that isn't satisfied just being comfortable or just getting by. This is a group that is on a completely different persistence path.

This persistence is about those looking to find their greatness. Those looking to explore their potential. Those desperate to squeeze every ounce of amazingness and possibility out of this short life.

This is a persistence of choice, not default. Of challenges chosen rather than avoided.

See, we all get to choose. None of this is preordained. Plenty of folks with far more tragic and traumatic and "hopeless" situations have chosen to persist in pursuing their greatness. They've chosen to leave the excuses and rationalizations and laziness at the door.

Regardless of where you come from or how bad it's all been, you get to choose, too.

Do you choose the persistence of survival, or do you choose the persistence of greatness?

I promise they're both hard in their own way. But only one of them will allow you to close your eyes that final time, knowing you did all you could, that you left nothing on the field, and that you cheated not yourself or any of the rest of us of your greatness.

Action Step

Realize you're not alone. Don't let appearances fool you. Know that everyone—no matter how good things might look—is struggling. There's comfort in this universality of experience.

Stop resisting challenges, pain, and heartache. Resistance is for amateurs and victims. Teach yourself to expect problems; they aren't stopping any time soon. The quicker you learn to embrace them, the quicker you'll get to work on solving them.

Understand that the worst stuff will, without question, be your very best teachers. These worst moments will **ALWAYS** come packaged with an even greater gift hidden inside the struggle. It's your job to dive in, do the work, and find that gift. (It might take weeks, months, or years for this gift to be revealed. Be patient.)

Remember that the better your skills, ability, and preparation, the better chance you have of navigating adversity with the least amount of pain and overwhelm.

Draw a line in the sand. On one side is surviving and just getting by. On the other is your potential, your greatness, your possibilities. You have to decide where you'll stand and which kind of life you wish to live. Both will require persistence and effort, but only one will reward you with the self-love and pride of knowing you never gave up on uncovering your very best self.

My Experience

Coming from a background that had some good-sized challenges built into it—as well as getting the regular life "surprises" and knock-arounds—I had plenty of moments where I was completely overwhelmed and sure I wanted to give up or take the easy way out.

I've been in such dark places, for such extended periods of time, that I'm often surprised I found my way out.

I've been hopeless, broken-hearted, homeless, penniless, family-less, and mentally and emotionally at the breaking point.

Unfortunately, much of this was my own doing.

My lack of skills and lack of personal work had left me extremely vulnerable and handicapped.

The holes in my personal development meant I set up many traps for myself. It also meant I was unable to avoid many of the traps I should have dodged.

Along with that, I had no positive framework or mindset to view these challenges through. So all I saw was the downside.

After discovering new influences, and after doing a ton of work on myself, I realized that all these "doom and gloom" moments weren't the world-enders I thought they were.

Through a different mental lens, I was finding that these troubles and challenges were the exact teachers I had always needed.

Instead of destroying me, I discovered that these moments were slowly molding me into a person of far deeper knowledge and understanding.

I began to see challenges as opportunities to grow. Or better put, demands for me to grow.

Instead of feeling beat down by life, I was looking at each time I stumbled as "school time."

When you can make that shift, you start to see obstacles and working through them in an entirely different light.

Persistence becomes less about drudgery and enduring, and more about developing.

I found that the things that I thought were my curses (emotional issues, relationship issues, learning issues, family issues), were actually my biggest gifts.

All the stuff I was certain had been holding me back, had actually been the very things pushing me forward.

My "specialness" and ability to connect came not from the easy times, but instead from the pain and challenges and unique circumstances I'd had to navigate.

Working through all my "stuff" has given me a unique ability to share these skills and insights with others—often in a way that connects when others can't. That's why I write. Why I teach. And why I'm driven to make a difference.

And speaking of making a difference, if this book is any indication, you should be able to see that I made a very conscious choice about which path of persistence I chose to walk.

For the first forty years or so, I chose the persistence of just surviving. And that's what I did. I survived. I got by. Barely.

I was so caught up in survival mode that helping and impacting others wasn't even on the radar. That's the tragedy of "survival persistence." You're so busy surviving that you're unable to be of any significant service to others.

When I made the decision to persistently pursue my potential, everything changed.

Yes, I still have all the same challenges and pains-in-the-rear that all the rest of us have, but I made a choice to ask for more. More challenges. More hurdles. More difficulties.

And why? Because deep down I knew I was better than what I'd shared previously. I knew there was more to me. I knew I was ready to take on far bigger challenges—to learn, to grow, and to persevere—to find my best self and to share whatever I found with the rest of the world.

{ Wrap-up:
The 24-Hour Book

For those of you who don't know the story behind this book, here's the quick overview—its origin story.

I've always felt that even in an ocean of self-help and self-development materials there'd always been something missing.

I'd always felt that there were two things that kept people from exploring this world. A world that actually **COULD** change your life.

One was trust. With so many opposing points of view—so many cheesy get-rich or get-happy-quick titles, and so many questionable characters, all vying for your attention and your dollars—trust is a scarce thing. I also hoped that making it not-for-profit would help.

The other was size and feel. So many of the great materials out there were either huge and overwhelming (books over 500 pages should be outlawed!), or they were written in an outdated fashion that made it hard for many to identify and connect with.

So, being the optimistic young man I am, I decided I'd fix all that. I decided I'd write a teeny, tiny, casual, nuts-and-bolts, zero-B.S. personal development book. The one I'd always felt was missing.

It would be written not by a millionaire, or fast-talking "guru". No, this little book would be written by a regular person who'd been through a fair amount of difficulties, who'd done most of it wrong for most of his life, but who had found a way out.

I wanted to create the book I'd always wished I'd had way back when.

I wanted to write a simple, believable, trustworthy book that might just help some others who were stuck.

Oh, and I decided to write it in 24 hours.

What's crazy is, I actually managed to do it. I wrote the entire basic foundation over one, very long, sleep-deprived 24-hour period. From there, I tweaked it a bit and, as is my style, I went into full-push mode.

I booked a trip to New Orleans to record the audiobook version, and spent 4 days getting it on tape. (Okay, digital.)

I'd also had a professional copy editor go over the book and make sure it was in typo and grammatical ship-shape.

Then I spent a little time letting it sit. I'm not sure why I didn't take the next steps to publish it (I'd already announced it was done), but sit on it I did.

I think I knew deep down that this book needed more. More time, more attention, more thought, more care.

This was, after all, not just some short story. This book was a mission. It had a purpose. I think I knew that if I wanted this book to help and impact in the fashion I'd hoped, it was going to require a lot more of me.

And so the 24-hour book turned into the 4-month book. Something I poured more into than I thought I had. I worked on average 4-6 hours a day. (Usually closer to 6.) It was easily the hardest thing I've ever attempted.

From a 24-hour lark, to something I was pretty sure I'd never finish. I don't think I can convey the difficulty and self-doubt these last 4 months entailed.

Why was it so hard? I've asked myself this question over and over.

My best answer is that in trying to condense down some of the most essential, transformative, deeply valuable principles into a few short pages and chapters, is a nearly impossible feat. And probably why so many of the other personal development books are so big!

The endless avenues, angles, points of view, examples, and sheer possibilities you could explore make the narrowing process an exercise in self-torture.

At least it was for me.

But somehow, some way, I managed. I actually finished this monster. Even though it's just a wee monster.

Something that helped me get through, especially on the days when I sat there for hours writing and re-writing a single paragraph that refused to not suck, was this phrase I told myself: Your worst version of this book, released, will help more people than the best version, you never share.

And so here it is. I know it's far from perfect. I know I'll look back in a few months and wish I'd said something more eloquently (or less so), added this or, for God's sake, not said that! But it is what it is.

It won't be for everyone. And that's okay. But for those of you that it connects with, I hope it serves you well, and I look forward to hearing from you.

Sean O'Shea

November 26th, 2017

The Resource List

Here's my top 25 guide to the book/audio/Internet/social media list. This is by no means a comprehensive list. There are zillions of other valuable materials out there just waiting for you if you're looking. Along with that, not all of these will (or are supposed to) resonate with you.

I've included a diverse collection of writers, speakers, and thinkers, in the hopes that you can be exposed to many different approaches and perspectives, so you can find what does and doesn't resonate with you. Personal development information is a highly personal affair. What works for me, or someone else you know, might not work for you at all!

My suggestion is to get online and do some research. Scope out free YouTube videos, read Amazon reviews, listen to samples on Audible. Your job is to find what speaks to you, where you are currently. Also, this will likely change over time as you develop and grow. That's totally cool. Allow it. Start with what makes sense now and see where you end up in a year or two.

That said, if you're overwhelmed by this list, my recommendation is to start with Jim Rohn's *Art Of Exceptional*

Living 6 CD set. This collection had (and continues to have) the biggest impact on my life. I've probably listened to this collection a few hundred times. Every listen reveals something new and, somehow, previously unheard! I recommend you listen to this no less than 10 times consecutively. And the more you listen, the better!

As your consciousness and knowledge grow, you'll find yourself finding more nuggets of wisdom and insights in the materials you explore. You'll hear things and understand things you missed the first, second or tenth time! So be prepared to revisit any of the books/video/audio that feel valuable somewhere later down the line. You'll be shocked how materials you study grow as you do.

(You'll likely also be embarrassed by where you used to be and how "evolved" you thought you were. I always am.)

And by all means, write all notes and ideas down that feel valuable. **DO NOT** skip this crucial step! Keep a journal or write directly in the book itself (my style!). This style and habit of studying will absolutely aid you in processing the material more deeply.

You'll understand it more, hold onto it more, and be able to access and utilize it more when you need to.

Also, as you read, listen, and watch, it's imperative that you develop the habit of pausing when an important idea or concept flashes across your consciousness. These are critical moments of insight and development. Or shall I say opportunities for them? Stop, contemplate, process. If you skip the pausing and reflection part, you'll miss many of these key, possible "aha" moments.

Interacting with material you're attempting to absorb (writing, thinking, speaking), has been shown to increase the retention and the understanding of the material dramatically!

Even though it's tempting, don't be in a hurry to get through the material. Just be focused on how much you can pull from it. Even if it takes you a month to read a book. One valuable book—carefully and consciously consumed, evaluated, and processed—will yield far more valuable results than five books read in a lighter fashion in the same amount of time.

Remember, you're teaching yourself new skills, new perspectives, and even new ways of thinking about life! This is seriously hard work. You'll need patience and tons of repetition. Don't shortchange yourself by being in a hurry.

Take your time, dive deep, explore the material—and yourself. I promise the deeper you dive, the better your results.

Books/Audio

1. *The Art of Exceptional Living* (6-disc set), and *The Challenge to Succeed* (2-disc set), each by Jim Rohn
2. *The Compound Effect*, by Darren Hardy
3. *As a Man Thinketh*, by James Allen
4. *The Success Principles*, by Jack Canfield
5. *Psycho-Cybernetics*, by Maxwell Maltz
6. *Awaken the Giant Within*, by Tony Robbins
7. *Leading an Inspired Life*, by Jim Rohn

8. *The Slight Edge*, by Jeff Olson

9. *The Power of Intention*, by Wayne Dyer

10. *Shut up, Stop Whining, & Get a Life*; *You're Broke Because You Want To Be*; *It's Called Work for a Reason*; *Your Kids Are Your Own Fault*; and *Grow A Pair*, each by Larry Winget

11. *Meditations*, by Marcus Aurelius

12. *The Little Gold Book of Yes Attitude*, by Jeffrey Gitomer

13. *Goals* (2-CD set), by Zig Ziglar

14. *Mindset*, by Carol Dweck

15. *How To Win Friends and Influence People*, by Dale Carnegie

16. *Think and Grow Rich*, by Napoleon Hill

17. *The War of Art*; *Do the Work*; and *Turning Pro*, each by Steven Pressfield

18. *Why You're Dumb, Sick and Broke*, by Randy Gage

19. *The Magic of Thinking Big*, by David Schwartz

20. *The Art of Happiness*, by The Dalai Lama

21. *The Gifts of Imperfection*; *Daring Greatly;* and *Rising Strong*, each by Brene Brown

22. *Tools of the Titans*, and *Tribe of Mentors*, each by Tim Ferriss

23. *The Richest Man in Babylon*, by George Clason

24. *The Icarus Deception*, and *What to Do When It's Your Turn*, each by Seth Godin

25. *The Obstacle Is the Way*, and *Ego Is the Enemy*, each by Ryan Holiday

Blogs & Social Media

- Seth Godin's Blog
  sethgodin.typepad.com
- Randy Gage's Success & Prosperity Blog
  www.randygage.com/blog
- Darren Hardy's *Darren Daily* email mentoring
  dd.darrenhardy.com
- Gary Vaynerchuck
  Facebook: *www.facebook.com/gary*
  Instagram: *@garyvee*
  YouTube: *www.youtube.com/GaryVaynerchuk*
- Casey Neistat's YouTube channel
  www.youtube.com/CaseyNeistat
- Dwayne "The Rock" Johnson
  Instagram: @therock
- The Tim Ferriss Show
  tim.blog/podcast
- Chase Jarvis' YouTube channel
  www.youtube.com/chasejarvis
- Eric Thomas' YouTube channel
  youtube.com/etthehiphoppreacher
- Tom Bilyeu's YouTube channel
  www.youtube.com/tombilyeu
- Marie Forleo
  YouTube: *www.youtube.com/marieforleo*
  Instagram: @marieforleo
  Email list: *www.marieforleo.com*

Acknowledgements

As always, there's far too many folks to mention to do this list any justice.

Instead of naming names, I want to simply say thank you to everyone that's been a part of my life in any fashion. You've all made me the man I am today, and for that I am eternally grateful.

I'd also like to send out a giant hug of appreciation to all those (past and present) willing to stand up, stand out, take chances, take the hits, and build a world you believe in. You inspire me daily to be a better man.

Above all else, I'm deeply thankful to have had a second chance at this life thing.

About the Author

Sean O'Shea is a world-renowned dog trainer, teacher, entrepreneur, and author. He splits his time between Los Angeles and New Orleans.

If this book has helped you in any way, Sean would love to hear from you. You can contact him by sending an email to sean.closingthegap@gmail.com.

You can also find Sean online at:

- TheGoodDogTraining
- @TheGoodDogTraining
- TheGoodDogTraining
- www.TheGoodDogWay.com